When We Were
Almost Like Men

When We Were Almost Like Men

Martin Hayes

STACK
BOOKS

Smokestack Books
1 Lake Terrace, Grewelthorpe, Ripon HG4 3BU
e-mail: info@smokestack-books.co.uk
www.smokestack-books.co.uk

ISBN 9780992958107

Smokestack Books is represented
by Inpress Ltd

Contents

problem solving

we sit at control points
on computers bought in job-lots
from the auctions of liquidated companies.
we sit at control points
using radio equipment
that 3-year-olds would consider
not to be worth the bother.
we sit at control points
having to repeat things over again and again and again
until the blood starts pounding inside our heads and necks
hoping that the rider down the other end of the line
is getting enough fragments of it enough
for it to make some sense.
we sit at control points
watching our computer screens
fill up with jobs
unable to get them out
because at any one time
it's either the radio that isn't working
or the software that's decided to crash
and at the end of the month
we pick up our performance related pay
and go down the pub
to celebrate Phoenix Express' new policy
of making it compulsory
that their controllers wear a shirt and tie
from now on.

after 14 years of putting up with this
it's a comforting feeling to know
that the eighteen-million-pound company we work for
hasn't lost any of its famed direction
and is still concentrating on the things
that really matter.

our dignity

working in control rooms
next to each other
we take the piss out of the clothes we wear
we take the piss out of our new haircuts
we sneak up behind each other
and pull levers under our controllers chairs
just as we're lifting scolding cups of coffee to our lips
we get our hands on photographs of each other's girlfriends
cut and paste their heads onto pictures of girls
shoving cucumbers up their cunts
then come in early to blue-tac them to the backs of our chairs
we leave messages on each other's answer-phones
telling the woman of the house
what a brilliant blow-job she gave last night
and that we hope he doesn't expect anything
we let each other's tyres down
and fill each other's petrol tanks with sugar
we call each other queers and pussies
and drive screwdrivers into the air-suspension pouches
of each other's chairs
we take magic markers with us into the bogs
and write about how our fellow controllers fuck their mothers
and suck off their children
drawing meter-high diagrams of the act
we package up bits of our shit in a box
and send it to each other's homes
we leave e-mail messages on each other's screens
cut so it seems to have been sent by the MD
telling us that we are to be sacked
at the end of the month
we take the Rentokil mousetraps dotted around the office
and slip them into each other's jacket pockets
we call our blood lines into doubt
and predict that our future kids
are so inbred

that they will be born
with at least one limb missing

the amazing thing is though
in the 16 years I've been a controller
not one of us has died at the hands of another

we like to leave that sort of thing
to the people in the offices upstairs
who don't seem to give a damn about a controllers dignity
or self-respect

hopeless cases

controllers are forever bemoaning the fact
that they get an unfair proportion of the blame
whenever the company loses a client.
they elect representatives
to attend management meetings
to stand up for them.
they continually fill out internal complaint forms
highlighting the uselessness of the software programme
they have to work with.
while they take a shit
they write with magic markers
what they really think about each other
onto the backs of the toilet doors.
they spike their supervisor's drinks with liquid MDMA
and come in early some days
to sabotage their fellow controllers computer set-ups,
swapping interface cards
and keypads
for ones on which the K and 4-key doesn't work.
they send anonymous celebration cards
to fellow controllers who have just been given two weeks' notice.
they send anonymous congratulation cards
to fellow controllers who have recently been diagnosed with
acute angina.

controllers like to think
that they are normal human beings
and that the only things that make them nasty
are other controllers.

rotating weathers

between 5 and 7 every afternoon
and between 7 and 9 every morning
the shifts change

those with bleary eyes walk in
saying nothing
and those with bright eyes
walk out
saying that there's a whole heap of shit
to sort out

but because this happens on a rotational basis
no one ever has bleary eyes for too long
or bright eyes
for long enough

keeping it together

the dilapidated hardware
and the tin-pot software
and the stuck-on-17-degrees air conditioner
that not even the engineer can fix

the power-crazed supervisors
and the egomaniacal controllers
and the amount of bodies
that have not been trained to do the jobs they have been given
and the customers
that swear and cunt at you
because their parcels have not been picked up
and the riders that think you're there
just to stitch them up
and the reps that come down
just to chew your ear
because their new account has been fucked-up
by one of the previously mentioned
and the telephonists
that just want an answer to tell the customer
that's screaming at them down the phone
which you can't give
because the rider's battery on his antiquated radio
has gone flat once again
all pales into insignificance
after your shift finishes
and you cycle home to your woman
and put the key in the door
not knowing what might be on the other side

because that's when
you've really got to try
to keep your shit together

how to be get singled out as a trouble maker

there is a computer set-up in the control room
under the power poster that proclaims
'problems are for internal meetings
not for customers ears'
that every time you punch they K-key too hard
causes the system to stutter, freeze,
then crash.

there is no note attached to this computer set-up
warning any user
not to punch the K-key too hard
as it can cause the system
to crash
and no supervisor has ever thought
of actually replacing the faulty keypad
because that is not in the rationale
of the company

it is also no good for any of us controllers
to suggest it
because that would just be considered
make believe
and single you out
as a trouble maker

the winner

at the end of his shift
Neville gets up from his chair
and after doing a hand-over to his replacement
hits the key on the keypad
that brings a job count up onto the screen

if it has been a good day
he mutters to all of the other controllers
about how many jobs he has covered
compared to them

if it has been a quiet day
he walks out without even a goodbye
saying nothing

but if it has been an extra busy day
he walks around the control room
pulling up the job count on the screens next to all of the other
controllers
standing back with his hands inside his pockets
waiting for you to look at him
so he can nod his head at the screen
just in case we were in any doubt about how good he was
before walking out
to get into his Ford Mondeo
and drive the 25-miles home
where he challenges his 6-year-old son
to anything he feels hot at
in the family collection
of Sony PlayStation games

once or twice a day

nothing got Neville, our highest paid controller, more
than a slow computer.
he'd update his screen
and if it took more than 3-seconds to unfold the new jobs
he'd get angry and start snarling
punching away at his keypad even harder than he usually did.
so when one of his fellow controllers
one busy Friday afternoon
slipped into the server room
to replace Neville's interface card with an inferior one
it was only going to be a matter of seconds
before Neville would once again get up from his controllers chair
and start announcing
that he was working for a Mickey Mouse company
and that it was doing his head in.

that Phoenix Express
had only two superior £500 interface cards
to go around eight control-points
that together generated near on
twenty-three-million-pounds worth of turnover a year
wasn't the point.

there is no point
other than to rattle the cages of people like Neville
at least once or twice a day.

a change of heart

when Neville was a controller
he used to join in on the banter
about us all being shoved up against it
with 4 fingers shoved up our arse
but still expected to keep the lids
on a thousand steaming pots
and a shot to fuck gas oven
and he used to fuck and cunt
along with the rest of us
at the way our performance related bonuses
were stopped
for things that weren't our fault
but just natural events
that the Mickey Mouse software we had to put up with
couldn't help but make happen
and he used to agree with the rest of us
as we sat near midnight in the pub across the road
drunk on cider and tequila after our 60-hour weeks
that it was the supervisor's fault
for dreaming up this 91% service level
and that having our bonuses stopped
for only achieving an 88% one
was not our problem

but now that Neville has been promoted to supervisor
suddenly it has dawned on him
that it is all our fault
after all

material

Susan
the little buxom 40-year-old Jewish Princess from sales
would come into the control room every now and then
wiggling her arse
and tell us about all the problems she was having
with her client base, with her children
with her Lexus-driving husband
and her Porsche-driving lover

she'd stand in front of you
with only the space
to slip a five-pound-note
in between you and her tits
and as she spoke
she'd watch your eyes
as you tried mammothly to keep them on hers
then when she finished she'd swing her wigging everything
around
walk out of the control room
and back up to sales

it was a shit job we all agreed
but it was great going home after all them hours
having something to actually think about

letting loose the hounds

the head telephonist
prowled around the telephonist room
looking for trouble.
she had a treble chin
and was fatter than Pol Pot on death.
she wore large flowery dresses
and painted her face black and red.
lips black eyes red.
she didn't do anything
but look over the shoulders
of all the underpaid telephonists
terrorising them
every now and then letting her big shrill voice
crack through their skulls.
they didn't know how to work the computer system properly
never mind keep a cool head.
when the controllers
noticed that a job had been taken down wrong
they had to go up to Janet to tell her about it
so she could then put the culprit right.
she was a fearsome creature though
and it was often easier
to just deal with it themselves
rather than let loose her hounds.

when Janet married the post room manager
of one of our largest accounts
she was moved up to sales
and we all felt
for our future customers
like we all felt
for our sanity
but could never seem to find it
while people like her were around.

doing something about it

I went into the recruitment office
to try and find out
why it was
that lately it seemed that we were getting
idiot after idiot
joining us as despatch riders

Patrick, the recruitment manager, was very nice about it
asked me to sit down
and listened to my various gripes
about the quality of the riders
he was taking on

after I'd finished
he thanked me for bringing this to his attention
and said that he would try to do
something about it

after my shift was over
I walked out into the courtyard
to find my pushbike
with both its tyres slashed

I was going have to realise
that even though we all worked under the same banner
there were some things
that just couldn't be said

the importance of law and medicine

every Summer
we get the sons of rich lawyers
surgeons, merchant bankers
dentists and university deans
come and join Phoenix Express
wanting to be couriers

the ones that want to be motorbike couriers
usually come with the best Rukkas under their arms
and top-of-the-range Arai helmets on their heads
while the ones that want to be cycle couriers
usually come with £1000 Cannondales under their arses
and the latest in trendy bright silks on their backs

for the first couple of days
they appear up-beat on the radio
and go around doing anything you give them
but after two or three weeks on the road
they think that they have learnt the ropes
and begin to bitch
questioning their controller's motives
demanding the same treatment
that the riders who have been through over 10 winters
getting lashed and drenched by wind and rain
getting undermined and constantly fucked-at
by aloof receptionists
and power-crazed post room managers
get

many of the sons of these great men
leave by the end of their first week
and go off to 'do' India or 'do' Thailand
and all of the rest
leave by the end of their first month
to go and study law
or get into medicine
which is what their Daddies had told them they'd only fund
them to do
in the first place

upgraded

the 5 or 6 career controllers we have
whose service records total in excess of 110 years
were forever reminding us 'boys'
about the processes that needed to be followed
and the regulations that needed to be adhered to
and despite the piss we took out of them
and the graffiti we put up on the bog walls
about them sucking the supervisors' dicks
they remained centred and unfazed
like they were following this great thing
that one day would deliver them

and whenever one of them got delivered
and made into a supervisor
the first thing he did
was send a memo around to all of the control room staff
telling us that he knew who was responsible
for the graffiti in the bogs
and that if it continued
then some heads were going to roll

well
at least it won't be our souls
you old cunt!

promotion

the ex-controller
recently made into a supervisor
walks around the control room
with his hands behind his back
trying to wear out his shoes
every now and then peering over us
and jabbing us in the back
asking us when we are going to cover 'that' urgent pick up
with a silver shirt and tangerine tie on
with a brand new company Vectra
waiting outside

when we ignore him
and huff at him
like he is just playing a part now
he puts us on report
for not showing him enough respect
and gets the company secretary
to write us letters of warning

supervisors
that have been promoted from controllers
are notoriously known
for their bad memories
and dress sense

the little souls

the souls of controllers

whose company have spent
hundreds of thousands of pounds
employing managers
whose sole task it seems
is to cut loose any dead or alive weight
it doesn't matter which
just so the company we all work for
can hit its 7% per-annum growth rate;
who walk around the control room in their £400 suits
explaining the latest internal complaint form designs
like it is the solution to all of our problems;
who sit in their leather pilot chairs
looking at figures on computer screens
and produce reports
explaining why our bonuses have been stopped
because we are only achieving an 88% service rate
rather than the 91% figure they've dreamt up;
who only breathe in real air
in the time it takes them to walk from their office
to their company car;
who've never had to fight back the thought
of committing suicide
and who've never had the bollocks to sack anybody
to their face;

have given up laughing
and now are just indifferent
that people can earn so much for having so little
in them.

futility

Phoenix Express require their controllers
to fill out report forms every time they finish a shift
report forms on which we are supposed to
list out any problems we have encountered
report forms on which we are supposed to
'elucidate' our opinions
and highlight any customer complaints we may have come
across
report forms on which we are supposed to
'speak frankly' about the working environment
we find ourselves in
but which we must keep our complaints
at an 'objective' level
and to not let ourselves get carried away
'by trying to right the universe'
report forms on which
we are supposed to sign our names
that no one will ever read
and which one day will be shredded
by people who will have to fill out report forms
on the efficiency of their shredding machines

someone somewhere at Phoenix Express
must know why and what they are doing
even if we don't

times are tough, don't you know

two months before Christmas
the telephonists attended a meeting
chaired by the MD
in which he told them
that he wanted them to be more motivated
and feel like an integral part of the company
rather than automatons that come in
and just go through the motions.

a week before Christmas
the telephonists were sent a memo from the MD
telling them that they wouldn't be needed
after December 24th
until January 5th
adding also that they wouldn't be paid
because, 'the economic environment was tough
at the moment.'

when they came back on January 5th
three of their representatives
asked their supervisor
if they could have a meeting with the MD
to ask him what he had meant
by wanting them to be motivated
and feel like an integral part of the company
rather than automatons who come in
and just go through the motions.

they were told by their supervisor
that they could have the meeting
but would have to wait four weeks
until the MD came back
from holidaying in the Cook Islands.

into the long stretch

the more years a controller has spent in a control room
the more paranoid and cynical he becomes
and the less likely he is
to talk to his fellow controllers

some controllers
have spent so many years in control rooms
that they think the mountains and stars
are just cardboard cut outs
and some have even given up talking to themselves
because they are frightened
that the bastard might just go ahead and tell everyone
what he is really thinking

the great trance

when you wake yourself up in the middle of the night
shouting out riders numbers
asking them whether they've got their details or not,
when you answer the phone 'Phoenix Express'
rather than the usual 'hello',
when you take walks through Regents Park
unable to tear your mind away
from office politics
or how secure your job might be,
when you sit down for dinner with your woman
only to be shouted at and amazed
that she has been talking to you for ten minutes solid
and you haven't caught a word of it,
when you go to the cinema
and immediately fall into a deep sleep
only to wake up when the lights come back on
happy at least that you had got away from it all
for a couple of hours
and when you stand in pubs with your mates
only to be nudged back from a great trance
and asked what the fuck is wrong with you
you know that you have finally crossed over the line
and that it will only be a few more years
before you won't be able to fall asleep
at all.

not having it

controllers
with faces lined with such disgust
that just don't want to be there

controllers
ignoring the gold-star urgent symbol
that flashes next to urgent jobs on their computer screens
making sure they do just enough
making sure they never get caught fucking up
pretending to themselves that they couldn't give a toss
not caring about the clothes they wear
not caring about their unwashed hair

controllers
who go around the control room
spouting off about imaginary girls that they fucked
the night before
or this new job they have been offered
with 6-weeks paid holiday
and an extra 10K per year

controllers
turning up
day after day week after week year after year
in the same office
in the same numb frame of mind
hoping that at some stage
the feeling will come back
and their minds will start beating again

déjà vu

whenever the hardware or software crashes
more than the 20 times a day
than it usually does
the management call in the priests.

the software priest comes in after lunch with one of the supervisors
and walks around asking us
'it can't be as bad as he says
can it?'
we invite him to sit with us
and to witness the build-up of work
and the way we have to move like lightning across the keypads
punching in commands
just to keep up with it all
and then the arbitrary stuttering and jerking
this system we have to rely on
is guilty of
before it crashes once again.

he leaves telling us
that it's obviously a hardware problem.

funny that
whenever the hardware priest comes in
he leaves telling us
that it's a software problem.

burying the guts

he had worked 18-years as a mini-cab controller
before coming to work for us
soon after he started talking about suicide
as a valid way out
rather than the occasional impulse
he had felt every now and then
and after he started wearing those
little skimpy netting t-shirts
that only just about covered his 53-year-old flopping tits
sitting there in his controller's chair
with his eighteen-stone-belly dripping out over his jeans
rolling his fat neck-head around on top of his spine
and shooting his eyes up into his head
every time it got busy
talking all the time
about what might be on the other side of the machine
suddenly standing up sometimes
and going over to everyone
and asking them to look at
how much his hands were trembling...

no one ever asked him
what he meant by what might be on the other side of the machine
and no one ever openly worried
why he might be trembling so

we knew
how much you could profit from burying the guts
that he was trying to show us

in between controlling jobs

we walk through parks feeling nothing
trying not to go home
where there is no love no wine

in between controlling jobs
we lay in our beds with our eyes shut
listening to everything going on outside
trying to remember old dreams
and forgotten bits of our mind
come back like lightning-bolts

in between controlling jobs
we row with our women
over alcohol or nappies
over cigarettes or food
while through us runs this feeling
that we should not be doing this
but we can't do anything about it

in between controlling jobs
we sit dumb-opened-mouthed
staring into the carpet
for hours
we look Hell in its eyes
trying to find a position for the uselessness we feel
that we have become

and then the moment we get employed again
we begin to feel our blood
start running through us again
and then soon after that
our women start letting us fuck them again
and then soon after that
we start walking naked around our flats
like we once again own them
happy that at last we have got back a destiny
that can be held in a pair of her hands
and that will keep our heads from screaming
all of the god-damn time

Rotherhithe Ronnie

our longest serving coordinator
whose sole job it was
was to spot any potential delays in the service level agreements
we had with our customers
then call them up
to advise them of the delay
used to like listing out all the fuck-ups
us controllers were guilty of
and he didn't mince his words as he
got down into the fucking and cunting

whenever he had a client on the phone
fucking and cunting at him
he'd swing his anger around at the offending controller
and leave him in no doubt
how useless he thought he was
at the job he was paid 14K per year more
than Ronnie

there was nothing left for us controllers to do
other than to invite Ronnie
to sit on the box
to see if he could do it
any better

half an hour later
the control screen began to seriously back up with jobs
causing a supervisor to come out
and remove Ronnie
from the box

he never lost any of that anger though
and the expletives kept pouring out of his mouth
every time he had
to deal with a problem
but we all knew now
that he knew
deep
down
that he just didn't have that skill
and couldn't quite keep the lids
on a thousand steaming pots
and a shot-to-fuck gas oven
quite like us controllers could

freedom

the self-employed cycle couriers said
that this was the most freedom that they'd ever had
while holding down a full-time job
as they didn't have to bow, jump or lick the arse
of some suited-up boss

the self-employed motorcycle couriers said
that this was the most freedom that they'd ever had
while holding down a full-time job
as they didn't have to bow, jump or lick the arse
of some suited-up boss

the self-employed van drivers said
that this was the most freedom that they'd ever had
while holding down a full-time job
as they didn't have to bow, jump or lick the arse
of some suited-up boss

and I think they all believed this
as they raced through the streets at ridiculous speeds
dodging trucks, busses, pedestrians,
evading death by millimetres
at least ten times a day,
so that the parcels they were carrying
for that same suited-up boss
that they were glad not to work for
arrived on time

undelivered from evil

when Yankee Seven-Two was sacked
for refusing to do one to many jobs
than could be tolerated
he came up to the office
and listened to the supervisor explain why
he had to go
then when the supervisor had finished
he hurled his helmet through the hatch at him
and threatened to fire-bomb the office
that upcoming weekend.

we came in the following Monday
expecting to see the burnt-out wreck of the office
only to find it all up and still running.

yet again
someone with big promises
had failed to deliver us
from evil.

under the fridge magnet

after eleven-hours spent in the saddle
dodging trucks, cabbies
busses and pedestrians
breathing in Esso's finest
trying to ignore
the snide comments of receptionists
whose packages have not arrived
on time
and whose lives now
will never be the same

after getting stuck in lifts
and sworn at by disgruntled art designers
computer programmers, advertising reps
printers, typesetters
and some of the most beautiful women in the world

the last thing you want to do

is to come home to find a note from your 3-year-long woman
pinned to the fridge under one of them smiley-faced magnets
telling you that she's left
because she considers you a loser

just exactly what it is we're up against

yes
the sun shall rise
once again

yes
walking under a ladder
is anathema to most

yes
the boat should not have sunk
with all of those people on board

and yes
the Gods
or whatever it is you call them
can be cruel

and yes
when you come out of a printing shop off Clerkenwell Road
after cycling your guts out
in time for the press
to find the one and only thing
you need and hate
most
in this world
gone

the space where you left it
blank
there in front of you
the snipped padlock in the gutter

you start to realise
just exactly what it is you are up against

don't leave us Lucile

Janet was the most experienced telephonist in the whole gaff.
she had been in the game over 20-years and
no one could show her anything
until Lucile joined the firm that is.
Lucile was 18, fresh out of college
and as beautiful as spark catching tissue.
on Lucile's second day
Janet pulled her in front of everyone
and told her that she was doing it all wrong,
that she was too excitable
and that she needed to calm down
and stop flirting with the male customers
if she wanted to remain in the employment
of Phoenix Express
adding as an afterthought
that she thought Lucille might be a tart.
Lucile just stood up and punched Janet
full in the face
causing Janet to fall backwards and down
with her arms spread out
taking a couple of computer screens with her
onto the floor.
they were both called into the head supervisor's office
and we were all rooting for Lucile
but when they came out
Janet headed back into the telephonist room
and Lucile headed for the front door.

we all let out a sigh
realising once again
that life and fire
will not be tolerated
almost anywhere
never mind at Phoenix Express.

someone had to pay

all the telephonists were in constant fear of Janet
the telephonist manager
because she patrolled her 18-stone frame
around the telephonist room
like it was an almighty.
even though she never got her hands dirty anymore
by actually answering the phone
she would still lean over the shoulders of all the telephonists
commenting on where they were going wrong
and how they should have done this
and that
and whenever a trainee telephonist got it wrong
more than once
she'd lay her words into her and when finished
lay some more into the telephonist who'd been assigned
to train the new recruit

that the telephonist given the responsibility
of training the new recruit
didn't get any extra pay
for the extra responsibility
didn't bother Janet
someone was going to have to pay
for the controllers
who out of her jurisdiction
continually took the piss out of her Hitler-soul
four chins
and Jabba The Hut body

our witches

when the wife of Mark
walked in on a red-hot-busy Friday afternoon
and screamed at him across the control room from the hatch
that he was a cunt for not coming home
for the last five nights
leaving behind as she left
a baby car seat on the hatch's ledge
containing a baby swaddled in blankets
that Mark had to go over and collect

when the baby started screaming and crying
at Mark's feet
six telephonists came in from the telephonist room
and gathered around the naughty father
cooing and pursing their lips
at the thing inside the car seat

it was busy
and it was difficult for the supervisor
to keep his controllers at work
and send the telephonists back to their stations
without seeming inhuman

the supervisor finally told Janet
head witch and telephonist manager
to take the baby out back
and look after it

Janet picked up the car seat
and all the other witches followed her
cooing and pursing their lips
at the beauty it contained

I guess it was a decent thing to know
that despite all the shit we produced
and despite all the lies we told
when it came down to it
our witches
could make sure
that our dysfunctional fathers
held down a living

dead faces and tired eyes

the telephonists come in with dead faces and tired eyes
to sit around their stations
trying to do as little as possible.
they talk to their fellow telephonists
about the nastiness of their men
and the way they suppose
their kids are worth all the shit
they put them through
in the end.

the telephonists come in with dead faces and tired eyes
every now and then answering the phone
taking down jobs
back to front
laughing at how important this seems to be
to all of us controllers
who now have to explain to couriers
that they have been run 20 miles
to pick up a job that doesn't exist,
laughing at how important their supervisor makes it seem
when they have put the phone down on bookers from 20-
grand-a-month accounts
because they didn't feel they needed to put up
with the tone of the booker's voice.

the telephonists come in with dead faces and tired eyes
saying yes to everything their supervisor says
just so they can get rid of her
and get back down to working out how much a month they
can afford
to spend on Janey from accounts'
Littlewoods catalogue.

at the shipyard

two weeks before Christmas
the management sent a memo to all of the telephonists
telling them that they wouldn't be needed or paid
between December 24th and January 5th
adding as an afterthought at the bottom of the memo
that they were sorry
but had to think of the bigger picture

three telephonists walked out on the spot
while the rest of them
tried to get us all to boycott the Christmas party
in solidarity

everyone one made a pact
and on the night of the Christmas party
twelve telephonists and forty-eight other people
turned up
thus proving
that the idea of suffering for a principle
was nowhere near as high on the list of employees at Phoenix
Express
as getting completely off your tits
for nish

real fear

whenever one of the 'ordinary' telephonists
comes into the control room
in baggy-kneed tracksuit bottoms
and Primark sweat top
to ask the controllers where 'this bike' is
or how long 'this bike' will be
they fool with them
they stare straight into their faces
before looking them up and down
then puffing out their cheeks
in an attempt to let them know
what they would like to do with their tired faces
and tired bodies
if only they weren't tied
to some nutter who got them up the duff at sixteen
before telling them
that if ever they can get away from their nightmares for a night
then they'd gladly take them out for a few beers
followed by a kebab
and a bit of intimacy up an alleyway somewhere

whenever one of the 'special' telephonists
comes into the control room
in buttock-hugging slacks
low cut v-neck jumper
and Wonderbra
with their hair and face all done up
smelling like they have taken care
over every square-inch of their bodies
to ask us where 'this bike' is
or how long 'this bike' will be
the controllers immediately bring up the in-question customer file
call the rider concerned
then explain at length
and in precise terminology

why the courier is running late
adding as they turn to leave
that if the customer won't listen to them
then to put them straight through to them
so they can put them straight

the controllers do not comment on her disastrous love life
or decline to suggest a bit of alleyway intimacy
because they are scared of her in some way
it's just in case she is in any doubt
about how mature a controller can really be
when confronted by things
they normally only ever get to wank over

bless him

the MD walks through the control room
every month
on the Friday morning just after we have been paid
patting us on our shoulders
telling us not to worry
about the faulty software
and tin-pot hardware
that seems to be the only things
that stop our performance related bonuses
getting passed each month because
'they are working on it'

the MD tells us
on his once a month walkabout
not to worry
about our bowels developing stress-related cancer
or our alcohol bill
or our 4-months-behind-rent-meeting down the council
or the greedy unfed mouths of our electricity keys
because
after the next financial year
the £18,000,000 per year company we work for
and that he owns
will be in a position to do something
about the flaking asbestos in the toilets
that we currently have to take a shit in

ghosts in the system

when we heard
that we had 8 new computers coming in
we naturally thought
that they would be made available
to the control room
thus solving the problems
that the supervisors and reps
kept digging us out for
and what the MD
kept stopping our performance related bonuses for
which was mainly for not covering the urgent jobs
in time enough
before the old computers crashed,
leaving them like ghosts in the system,
as we waited twenty minutes for them to re-boot
which they had to do twelve times a day
on average.

when the new computers came in
the IT guys
carried them up the stairs
through the control room,
like boiling toffee passing under our noses,
and away into the reps' and supervisors' offices.

It wasn't going to get any easier
that was for sure.

no chart for that

there was no way
we were going to inject any change
while the son of the MD
was learning the ropes
as office manager

he came straight from the London School of Economics
to supervise
us

our controllers' meetings
were suddenly filled with graphs and charts
that he told us
gave a truer insight
on how we had been performing

Dermot didn't tell him
that it was his Dad's tight-fistedness
that had helped create his stress related bowel cancer
and Alex didn't tell him
that it was his Dad's insistence
that he worked three Saturdays per month
that had helped make his Tina decide to split with him
and Corey didn't tell him
that it was his Dad's managers
and their chaotic shift-pattern they'd assigned him
that had caused his slow debilitating dive into insomnia
and the rest of us didn't tell him
that it was his Dad
who'd helped create this drink and drug problem we all seemed
to have developed
since we had begun working for him

we didn't tell him
because there's no chart
for that

prime directives

the message that leaked down to us
from the January management meeting
was that the controllers were in
for a kick up the arse

for too long
apparently
we had been letting the bike riders rule the roost
at the expense of the prime directive
which was to satisfy the customers
who ultimately paid our wages

one by one
the supervisors pulled us in
and gave it us with both barrels

the following day
they got the company secretary to document the 'new way'
and create a memo
which she handed out to each of us
as we started our shifts

Mark stapled his copy of the memo to the front of his shirt
and walked around like a robot for the rest of the day
Danny made his into an aeroplane shape
and drew swastikas on its wings
Ronnie put a lighter under his
and let little bits of it float off into the atmosphere
while the rest of us
just crumpled them into a ball
and chucked them into the dustbin
where the rest of our prime directives
seemed to have ended up

our mechanic

at the end of his shift
he comes up to the control room
in his oily dungarees, unwashed hair and 5-day-beard
to enquire who's coming for drinks

on Mondays
and Tuesdays and Wednesdays and Thursdays
most
say no
or else make excuse

he leaves
calling us all tossers
or little soft scaredy-cat controllers

those controllers who occasionally say yes
usually turn up the following morning
in various states of distress
and dying eyes
while downstairs
he saunters around the workshop
slapping people on the back
telling them that no one can hold a drink
like their mechanic can

games

Horse the mechanic
likes to phone up the control room
and tell us that the rider we've been telling him we need
so desperately for the last hour
is going to be another couple of hours in the workshop
because Horse has dropped his bike on the floor
and cracked its exhaust pipe
while trying to drink a can of cider
and smoke a joint

after we have made phone calls to clients
telling them that their jobs are now going to be late
due to an unfortunate accident
Horse gets back on the phone
and tells us that he has made a terrible mistake
that the bike is in perfect working order after all
and that he hopes he hasn't caused us too much
trouble

levels

on the top floor
you had the offices of the MD and sales reps
with their brown and cream decor
executive toilets
and 45-foot-long mahogany-soaked boardroom

on the next floor
you had the hive of the telephonists
with their banks of computer screens
with the pictures of their many children
blue-tacked against their borders
and the control room
with all its flashy computers
that went down
as often as our performance linked wages

and on the bottom floor
you had Horse
running around with cider in his veins
running around with a fuel-tank on his head
and his pecker out
not trying to keep the bikes on the road
but always somehow
managing to

innocent

after it was recognised
that we had eight bikes in the workshop
that should've been back on the road by now
I was sent by the supervisor
down to the workshop
to find out why
they weren't answering their phone

as I descended the stairs
I smelt the pungent smoke and heard Cobain pounding out
and when I walked in
the eight riders that should have been on the road
were all holding hands
and dancing around in a circle
as Horse
sitting in a corner
filling out one of the many forms
looked up at me and just shrugged
as though he had had nothing to do with it

confidence

every now and then
we are sent by one of the supervisors
down to the workshop
to find out how long a particular rider will be
before his bike is ready to go back on the road

as we descend the stairs
down to the workshop
we can smell the smoke
rising up from the basement
and then when we walk in
everyone is holding hands
and there is some Seattle band pounding out

we look around for somebody to ask...
then Horse jumps out
as if from nowhere
with a gear system in his hands
and a tyre around his neck
telling us not to worry
that everything
as far as he can see it
is going according to plan

perspective

the supervisors tell us
that we shouldn't be so cynical
when we talk about the capabilities
of our mechanics.
we highlight the many incidents
and they still tell us
not to be so cynical.

meanwhile,
Horse sitting in his dentist's chair
swigging on a can of cider
tells everyone that comes into his workshop
that the world has already ended
and that the spoofs he is the instigator of
are high art
designed to cut away the self-importance
of all the cynical systems
that have destroyed the GUTS
of
all
the
men
in the world.

taking the bull by the horns

Horse called up the control room
and asked how the bike was doing
collecting the gear and brake system he needed
from Slocombe's in Neasden
for his Superbike
which the company had agreed to sponsor
in more ways than one

we told him that his request
had been put on low priority
and that the supervisor had told us
to cover it when we can
which we hadn't been able to do
as of yet

Horse put the phone down
and it was 20-minutes later
before we heard
that he'd commandeered a bike that had four urgent packages
on board
to drive up to Slocombe's
and get that gear and brake system
that made the world spin
the way Horse liked it to

recruitment policy

as we sat there
with sub-standard machinery
and a software package
that crashed every time someone stamped their foot
constantly trying to dig ourselves
out of holes and
lying to all and sundry as we
circumnavigated the truth and lied
to the supervisors
who in turn lied to the customers as we
created plausible excuses
for the fact of just being inundated with work
not being able to talk to our riders
because the radio had fallen off-line
once again
not being able to give the telephonists and supervisors
the answers they needed
as it all crashed down around us
as the lies started flying about
as the protection of the back became paramount
Horse
downstairs in the workshop
was recruiting for the annual paintball fight

the annual paintball fight

when Horse roped us in for the annual paintball fight
we didn't realise that we were going to have to be
up at 6.30 to catch the coach taking us down to
just outside Sevenoaks
and we didn't realise that we'd have a coach
stacked with cases of Stella
or that there'd be spliff after spliff passed around
all generated by Horse
or that a few of Horse's paintball mates
would be offering us microdots as we hit the A46
that skirted us around Sevenoaks
we didn't even consider
that the paintball place
would be closed due to a lack of interest
as the notice on the door said when we got there
we knew
that when you go out with Horse
you never get there

duckshoot

whenever Horse passed through the control room
he liked to walk the whole length of the control desk
flicking the backs of our ears
telling us with each hit
how useless he thought us to be
sat in them big controllers chairs
and how cute and forlorn we looked
trying so hard not to go under
when it was just plain obvious
considering the dilapidated hardware
and tin-pot software
that we didn't have a chance

'just waiting to be shot out of the water
by the big boys with 12-bores'

adding as he left
that he sure hoped none of us had a woman and kids
relying on us bringing home a pay-cheque
at the end of the month

censorship

during Ramadan
Horse came up into the control room
and waltzed around with a half-eaten kebab dripping from his
hands
going up to all the muslim controllers and telephonists
and pulling faces at them
as he sucked big greasy strips of meat up
into his mouth
telling them that it was great not to believe in a God
that we were all damned anyway
and how lovely it was to be damned
but to not care
turning around in front of them
holding the kebab above his head
whirling like a dervish
the chilli sauce and grease flying off him
as he forgot the muslims
and started shoving it in everybody's face
telling us all that
God doesn't exist
because *we* don't exist
stuck in our 11-hour-shifts
talking about last night's tv
making plans for rainy days
voting
buying microwave meals
pretending we are not ghosts
stuck in the system
papering over our isolation
with two-bob motives
and misplaced tolerance
before walking out
and chucking what was left of his kebab
through the hatch
so that it hit Janet the telephonist manager
on the head

after the enquiry
Horse was banned from having any alcohol in the workshop
and from coming up into the control room
for a whole month

violins at dawn

whenever the controllers get pissed
about their bonuses being stopped
or because they have to hold on an extra un-paid hour
because the cover hasn't been organised well enough
by the supervisors
even though they have been stopped pay before
for notifying them that they were going to be an hour late
due to an eviction notice meeting
down the council,
whenever the controllers begin to talk
about them being the only ones victimised
and held responsible for things
that they've notified their supervisors about
countless times before
but which they have not had the will or power
to implicate
Horse starts holding this imaginary violin up to his neck
over which he moves his right hand
and makes a sad face.

our head mechanic

likes to judge the new riders
by showing them his porn collection
which he keeps under the workbench
that the new riders have to sign their vehicle contracts on.

as they're reading the small print
Horse leans down
and throws onto the workbench
magazines showing women
shoving cucumbers up their cunts.

if they wince and turn away
then Horse gives them one of the old dog-bikes
that have been around the clock a couple of times
and are begging to die
but if they laugh and ask to see more
then Horse gives them one of his better models.

Horse is trying to cultivate
a fleet of perverts
and treats any comment on equality
with the middle finger of his right hand
firmly up.

on Horse

Horse used to like telling anyone new
about the time he fucked his sister
under a bridge covering Sydney harbour
and how all the women he'd ever fucked since
had never quite done it for him.

this got Horse a lot of flak from the people
but some of us non-people
knew it was just a shock tactic of his
and would ask him if ever her warts got in the way
to which he'd prickle for a moment
look at you,
trying to judge whether you were being disrespectful or not,
then let out this roar of laughter
straight from his gut
the moment he realised that you were as willing not to care
as he was.

the people are not like this
they would rather pick flowers than grow them
and that's why they never meet people like Horse
who can keep your head afloat sometimes
when it would be so much easier
to let it sink.

getting a service

after Yankee Six-Three
had complained directly to the supervisors
about the four hours it took
for the mechanics to give his bike a service
even though it had been booked in
and even though he had been promised on the day he started
that all services
would take an hour tops
Horse took the workshop's most powerful nail gun,
the one with 1000lbs of pressure per-square-inch,
and thrust it up against Yankee Six-Three's throat
just in case he was in any doubt
about the way he was to go about things
from now on.

lonesome cowboy

despite his performance record
which was ridiculously perfect
considering the antiquated tools and machinery
he had at his disposal,
despite his ability
at keeping everyone up
and enthused,
despite his encyclopaedic brain
which could define an engines problems
merely by the sound of its revs
and despite his jokes and banter
which seemed to be the only things that kept us sane
most of the time
the management decided to give Horse notice
after it was reported to them
that he had broken Kilo Three-Eight's hand in a vice
for calling him a cowboy.

french-kissing the wind

as we scrimped and saved for
the holiday in Tenerife as we
scrimped and saved for the electric bill as we
crawled the walls and let out our screams
while laying in a bed
listening to the piercing sirens as we
let the woman begin to pull apart our integrity
and felt our minds begin to dissolve as we
tapped at buttons and learned how to make
a force-field for our backs as we
developed various addictions
so that we could stick it all in a freezer for hours
hoping that it may never thaw
Horse
sat on his Slingshot
doing 145-miles-per-hour
through a built up area
french-kissing the wind

how to waste 220-grand and a company Merc

after a sales manager
and three new sales staff
were poached from a rival company
we were let known
that Phoenix Express had a new found direction
by the introduction of 'power posters'
hung on the walls of our control room.

'A HAPPY CUSTOMER
EQUALS A SECURE WORKFORCE'

'IT COSTS 5 TIMES AS MUCH
TO OPEN A NEW ACCOUNT
AS IT DOES TO KEEP AN EXISTING ONE'

'PROBLEMS ARE FOR INTERNAL MEETINGS
NOT FOR CUSTOMERS EARS'

it all looked very smart
but it didn't stop the computer system crashing
at least twelve times a day,
and it didn't stop the rain leaking in
every time the guttering on the roof
became blocked,
and it didn't alter the fact
that we had too many untrained operators
in highly skilled positions
or
that we were unable to keep hold of experienced couriers
because their mileage rate was set to low.

but at least the 220k increase in the wage bill
and the 35-grand company Merc for the new sales manager
made the MD feel
as though he was finally doing what we had always asked
by throwing money
at the problem

which was nice.

getting serious

in the three months
since the new sales force has been in residence
we have been treated to 'power posters'
telling us how important customers are,
the introduction of weekly 'motivation' meetings,
new coloured internal complaint forms
and numerous bollockings
from a sales manager in a Top Shop suit
who doesn't even know where Dean Street is
never mind ever sitting on a faulty operating system
for 11-hours straight.

it's no good any of us going into the MD
and telling him that he can't be serious,
that all he needs to do
is buy 5 new PCs
with higher-spec processors
than the ones we currently have.

after all
he wouldn't have committed himself
to an extra 220k on the wage bill
and a 35K company Merc for the new sales manager
if he wasn't serious
would he?

addressing the problem

as part of the 'new push'
Phoenix Express have invested £6,000
on a new personnel brochure
full of 'power slogans'
and 'family tree' charts
which are supposed to explain
at all points along the service chain
what we are supposed to do
and who we are supposed to call
if ever we are in any doubt
about making a decision.

it is printed on thick glossy paper
and has portrait photos
of all the supervisors and managers
who are the ones we are supposed to call
if ever we are in any doubt
about making a decision.

these are the same people
who decided to spend £6,000
on a new glossy personnel brochure
rather than the 4-grand it needed
to buy 5 new PCs with faster
more reliable
processors
which could make our operating software
at least adequate enough
to cut our problems
by 80%.

but then if that happened
I suppose you wouldn't need so many managers
sitting around on 60-grand-a-year salaries
addressing the problem.

guts, and guts alone

after Manni put the phone down on One-One-Eight
top-face and highest earning pushbike rider
for calling him a wanker
because Manni wasn't giving him as many jobs
as the previous controller
who had recently been sacked for his blatant favouritism
One-One-Eight got on the radio
and started spouting off to Manni's right-hand man
that Manni was a wanker
and that if he ever put the phone down on him again
then he was going to come up to the office
and rip his fucking head off.

after Manni's right-hand man told him this
Manni pulled him off the box
put the headphones on
and told One-One-Eight over the radio
so everybody else could hear
that if he ever wanted to do something about it
then he was there from 8 till 6 every fucking day
and that the monotonous hours he'd spent listening and
putting up with
the bullshit
that self-important receptionists and
power-crazed post room managers and
people like him liked
to throw about
had made him thirsty for a little death
and that he would relish the chance of going one on one
with him
anytime
finishing off by repeating his home address
three times over the air
'just in case you're a sneaky cunt'

One-One-Eight declined to pick up his pay cheque that Friday
choosing to call the pay roll department instead
to change his payment method to BACS
thus proving
once again
that the world doesn't just begin and end
with natural disasters
but sometimes by guts
and guts alone

comfort

the people that walked in after the take over
tried to soften the blow
of 40% of the workforce
getting made redundant
and the reduction of our lunch breaks
from 60 minutes to 30
and the planned gradual decline
of the new company contributions
into our PAYE pension packages
by offering all of us that were left
flight-jackets with the new company logo sewn into our
breasts
for a reduced fee
of only 44-pounds

the new church across the road

across the road from the operations room
over in the new sales and accounts building
it has been reported
that they never run out of toilet paper, sellotape
or air.

it has also been reported
that they have an air conditioning system
that never lets the temperature drop
from a cool solid 24-degrees
and that they have a water cooler and a coffee machine
and that it is populated by perfect looking people
dressed in suits
who walk around on £28-per-yard gun-metal-grey carpet
surrounded by forgiving apricot-coloured walls
under sunken spot-lights.

it is well known
that the new accounts and sales building across the road
has received more investment in the last year
than any of the other departments within Phoenix Express
put together.

it's even been rumoured
that they are going to build a steeple on top of it
just so they can make it a taller building
than the old church across the road.

when we were almost like men

before the new sales people were brought in
four of the five parking spaces in the company courtyard
were given up to first come first served
and those that had cars
used to gun their 79 Corollas and 83 Escorts
down the streets that led into the office
bibbing their horns
driving side by side
and whenever a van or bus loomed up the other way
they'd slam on their brakes
before slipping into the slipstream
of the rust-bucket in front
and when the turning into the road that led into the courtyard
came up
they'd attempt overtaking patterns fit for Gods
bumping up on pavements
trying to avoid bollards
swinging their steering wheels around their necks
cutting up anything that got in their way
and whenever one of them was successful
they'd immediately slam on their brakes the moment they
  entered the courtyard
holding everyone else up behind them
so that a convoy slowly formed
as they all let their £750 machines
purr down the hill at under 10-miles-per-hour
with all of their horns blaring
and the winners sat up in their bucket seats
their heads stuck out of their home-cut sun-roofs
pumped-up and screaming obscenities into the air
as they steered their tanks into that space
that meant so much
and then got out
brushing themselves down
striding towards the door into work
feeling almost like men

but now that all five parking spaces in the courtyard
are reserved for the MD and four new sales staff
the glory of the run has ceased
and most now just get the bus

give us sellotape

the head supervisor telling us
that we couldn't have a new reel of sellotape
because of cutbacks
followed the day after in a controllers' meeting
in which the same supervisor explained to us
that the company we worked for
had just committed themselves to a new 220k sales force
and that if we thought we were insignificant before
then we'd better hold on to our hats
because we were about to feel what it was like
to be employed by a 'real' organisation
that won't even pretend to give a fuck
about any of us
if we are found to be responsible
wasn't such a surprise
to any of us

we knew
that even if this company that we worked for
had just given us the 220-grand
and told us to have a good time
it wouldn't have made any difference
because it is well known
on the streets
and on the corners
and on the bottom of the sea
that sellotape is a valued commodity
amongst people whose lives are falling apart

cheap enough not to kill

the man from Rentokill
comes around every other Wednesday
to re-lay the old traps
and to lay down new ones.
we tell him that he must be on the side of the rats
because as far as we are concerned
the rats are just getting larger
and more plentiful.
he tells us that he told The Man
that this stuff he's laying
has only a 62% kill ratio
but that The Man chose it
because it was £37.50 a week cheaper
than the 92% stuff.
for all the Buddhist controllers
it was the first time they had ever come out
and agreed with the management's policy of cost cutting
but for the rest of us
it was just another sign
that not killing rats
was more important
than killing us.

take a break

you could rarely work out what was going on outside
sat in those big controllers chairs
staring into all of those computer screens
with all the slatted-blinds-snapped-shut
and the air conditioning stuck on up.

sometimes a window might be left open
and a breeze would pass over you
and sometimes a shaft of sunlight might slip through
and lay there on your hand for a moment
and sometimes the rain would be heavy enough
to make a noise up against those big 20-by-20ft windows
that in Summer baked our guts to gush.

but when our breaks came
we'd go outside and let the sun or rain
just
hit
us.

we wouldn't have been able to go back
or on and on
if it hadn't been for all of those 20-minute breaks
when we were able to turn our heads up to the sky
and run our fingers through our hair
feeling like something other
than what they wanted us to feel.

the moaners

we put up with hardware bought in job-lots
from the auctions of liquidated companies

we put up with software
written in Mickey Mouse language
and two weeks paid holiday a year

we put up with no sick pay
and toilets that have been shut down countless times before
by the health and safety officer
who gets called in by anonymous employees
every time they feel they have been mistreated

we put up with a leaking roof
and a stuck-on-18-degrees air conditioner

we put up with the many 'power posters'
that the new sales force have put up
in our control room
telling us that problems are for internal meetings
and not for customers ears

we put up with not being paid overtime
covering wankers who can't get in on time
even though we have been stopped pay before
for notifying them that we are going to be an hour late
due to an eviction notice meeting down the council

in fact
the only thing we can't put up with
are the people that come into work
moaning
thinking that this situation
we all find ourselves in
is not worth laughing about

now that
really got on our tits

motivation Harry's way

at our beginning of the week motivation meeting
Harry, our head supervisor,
tells us that the thousand and one ways
he uses to put down and humiliate
us controllers
are not just pulled out of a hat willy-nilly
but high art
handed down through the centuries
from supervisor to supervisor
taken from a big black book
originally written by the Great Supervisor Beneath The Ground
and that we are not the first
to think them unfair and totally unjustified
or to think about leaving
our £400-per-week controlling jobs
for ones in which we will not be treated merely like school-kids
adding as we got up from our chairs
that he didn't even give a toss if we did leave
because he could replace each one of us with a potted plant
and still raise the intelligence level in the control room
one-hundred-fold.

we knew that when we went out there
we were going to do our stuff
supervised by a man
with messianic delusions of grandeur
and that it would be best
to drop the four microdots that we had planned
into our leader's coffee
sooner
rather
than
later.

keeping them on their toes

the controllers first started spiking the supervisors' drinks
with speed and crushed sleeping pills
and we used to sit back and laugh
at the way the supervisors' mannerisms would change
on each circuit they took around the control room.

it wasn't long before they we were putting E
and liquid MDMA in there.
we were responsible for all their half-days
and reduced holiday pay.
then one day
Marcus decided to dissolve 4 microdots into Harry's coffee
and an hour-and-a-half later
two ambulance men arrived
to take Harry away.

after that
the supervisors bought themselves their own percolator
which they kept on top of the filling cabinet
inside their office.

it may have been childish and irresponsible
but at least they don't finish off their bollockings anymore
with the words, 'and while you're thinking about it son
get and make me a coffee.'
and at least whenever somebody does a coffee run now
they can walk past the supervisors' office
and lean in as they go past
to give them that knowing glance
that means so much
and tells them
that despite everything
we haven't lost all control
just yet.

Tyson

Harry, our head supervisor
had to come in once during the Christmas break
just to check that the wheels were still spinning
that the machine was still oiled
and that the staff were attending to their duties.

when he came in
we told him that a recently sacked driver
had been waiting in the reception area all day
refusing to leave
until he had got his deposit money back
which he thought was due him.

we didn't tell Harry that the recently sacked driver
had his pet pit-bull called Tyson with him
which we had all been admiring from a distance
so when Harry told us
to show him into his office
so that he could explain to him
that there wouldn't be any money
until the accounts re-opened on January the 5th
it must have been a big surprise to Harry.

and when the man walked out 8-minutes later
waving three pink £50-notes of Harry's in the air
with Tyson by his side
followed later by a Harry
that we had never seen before
it gave us all hope
that the rules as prescribed by Harry
were not going to stop some people
from achieving what they thought was just.

'told yer so, didn't I'

I was asked by Harry
to phone up Yankee Five-Six,
a veteran courier of ours
who had hardly missed a day
in of over fifteen-winters
but who unusually for him
hadn't turned up to work
for three days,
to find out what was going on.

Yankee Five-Six
told me that he had developed these strange pains in his chest
over the weekend
and on Monday had gone to see his GP
who sent him straight to the hospital for an ECG
and that he had got a call back that afternoon
telling him that he had
acute angina
and that he had been booked into St Mary's that upcoming
weekend
for heart surgery.

I went to tell Harry
the score
and the first thing he said was
'yeah, right,
next minute he'll be telling you that he can't come to work
because he's dead.'

the Monday following
a man phoned me up claiming to be Yankee Five-Six's Dad
and told me that his son had died
on the operating table
and could I arrange for someone to come around
to collect his radio
and company bike.

I went to tell the Harry the score
and the first thing he said was
'told yer so, didn't I.'

my family

the supervisor tells me that he wants me to be
more positive,
that he doesn't want to hear me
muttering negatives about the hardware,
the software, the riders, the telephonists
and the mechanics.

the supervisor tells me that he wants me to imagine
that all of those negatives
are my very own babies
that I have to nurture
into adulthood
and that ticking them off all of the 'god damn' time
creates a bad atmosphere
in which they cannot breathe
and cannot grow.

when the supervisor
has finished with his psychology lesson
I walk back out into the control room to do my stuff
only to find
that the software has crashed
again,
that the hardware is emitting smoke from its vents
and a rider at the hatch
shouting at me across the control room
that he knows where I live
and that I'd better watch my back
if I don't start giving him as much work
as the previous controller.

the lucky ones

when our head supervisor has nothing to do
he likes to come out into the control room
and terrorise the new recruits.
he likes to stand over them
letting them know that he is breathing down their necks
winking at us
every now and then pulling them up on a technicality
before retreating back into his office
and getting one of the telephonists
to make him a cup of coffee.

the new recruits are in a state of terror anyway
what with being thrust in front of a computer system
that they've had only two days training on
but it doesn't stop them trying
and the more they try
the more our head supervisor likes to come out
and tell them where they are going wrong.

sometimes when he is sat next to one of the new recruits
he swings his head around
and shouts over to the rest of us
that doesn't think this fella
is going to make it,

which wouldn't be such a bad thing
considering that if he did
then he might end up losing his fire and dignity,
become a drunk,
spend money he doesn't have on coke,
get bombarded with eviction notices,
develop stress related symptoms
and sometimes think about committing suicide

just like
the rest of us.

justice

three days before the monthly controllers' meeting Tim
the elected representative for us spineless bunch of yellow men
comes around with his notebook and pen
to ask us how we are doing and whether
we want anything in particular raised
at the upcoming monthly controllers' meeting.
we tell Tim
that it doesn't matter what's raised
because it will all just continue cartwheeling down the hill
and the computers will still crash the fifteen times a day
that they usually do
and we will all still have our bonuses stopped
for reasons that aren't our fault
and we'll still find rat droppings in the kitchen
and we'll still have to continue working
with inferior communications equipment
and we will all still be threatened with the sack
by supervisors who have less of a hold on reality
than we do.

Tim then tell us
not to be so cynical
and for the thousandth time
about his grandad
whose union representatives
through diligence and persistence
forced British Steel into paying out a five figure sum
and admit in a court of law
that it was their faulty ventilation equipment
that contributed to his grandad
losing the use of both his lungs.

as controllers
we didn't have any machinery around that smelted ore
and we didn't have to worry about losing a limb
or the use of a lung
all we had to worry about was losing our minds
and we avoided that
by every now and then sticking a screwdriver
into the tyre of a supervisor's car
or spiking a supervisor's coffee
with liquid MDMA.

that was our
justice.

nothing in your corner but a bust mouth and a shat on soul

when we heard that an old rep of ours
had his house fire-bombed by his new company
just to warn him off the threat he levelled
at his redundancy meeting
which was something along the lines
of him going into all of their accounts
and trying to poach them

when we heard that an old controller buddy of ours
had shot himself in the wrists
just to relieve the pressure that was being placed on him
by the job and kids

when we heard that all telephonists
were not going to be needed or paid
for the two weeks over Christmas
effectively laying them off
despite the other fifty when we relied on them
and despite their rents still having to be paid

and when we heard
that all pay queries were on hold
until the MD came back
from his winter break in the Cook Islands
and that there was no use all of us
continually going on about the shit software
that crashed every hour
causing us to lose our bonuses
as though it was some sort
of petty excuse

we finally realised
that only one thing was going to save us
and that we didn't have the guts
to do it

we have failed at everything, but this

we can't do it any other way

we have failed at everything
but this

we have tried selling drugs
we have tried living on the dole
we have tried being self-employed
we have robbed strangers and stolen our own mother's jewellery

we have tried to drink our way through it
we have tried smoking and injecting our way through it
we have tried running away from it
and we have tried running towards it
with all of our arms open

we have been asleep in alleyways
and asleep in beds
with a woman spooned into us

neither of them work

we've even tried ripping out all of the phone wires
and bolting up all of the doorways
and we've seen all the lying films
and read all of the beautiful books

but nothing ever seems to do it as good
as the night when you've just finished your 60-hour-week
  controlling job
and go back to your flat with a bag of wine under your arm
only to crack open a few
sitting at your open window
staring dumb-eyed into the sun-setting-sky
trying not to let yourself dribble from the corners of your mouth
at the taste of such freedom
and the knowledge that you owe everybody in the world
absolutely
nothing

through the door that's always open

whenever I ask Harry, our head supervisor,
why it is that Phoenix Express insist that we do certain things
in their particular way
even though that way has been proved time and time again
not to work
and that doing it that way
causes us controllers to lose our bonuses
and sometimes even clients
he looks at me as though I am mad
then looks over my shoulder
and pretends to notice something off in the distance
that needs his urgent attention
telling me as he gets up and walks away
that he hopes he'll not have to fire me one day
for not just getting on with it

Interflora and tragedies

when a new controller starts at Phoenix Express
he is told by the supervisors
that their door is always open
and encouraged to come in anytime they want to talk to them
about any problems they might have
or might see
potentially arising.

controllers that have been there for over 6-months
are let known regularly by their supervisors
that their doors are firmly shut
and that any problems they might have
or might see potentially arising
had better not come back to their fucking doorstep
if they want to keep hold of their fucking jobs.

this is why when supervisors get hospital stays
or their daughters raped
they sign the company 'get well' or 'condolence' card
but still manage to drum up their own version
in which they write
'we hope you die soon, you fuck'
or
'don't be sad, he only did what you wanted to do,
you nonce'
before one them going down to an un-local florist
attaching it to a wreath
and paying for it to be delivered to his ward
or family home.

it's a good job that tragedies and Interflora exist
otherwise they'd never get to tell the fuckers
what they really think
about them.

the new controller

they didn't know what to make
of the new controller
what with her blonde hair
long legs
and killer blue eyes.
when the supervisors brought her out
and introduced her to them
they didn't know what to make
of the new controller.
they didn't know whether it was a joke
or a test.
they got even more confused
when they sat her on the push-bike box
and she proceeded to control it
for the whole afternoon
effortlessly.
then when she was put on channel 2,
our third busiest circuit,
they just sat back and waited
for the log-jam to arrive,
but it never came
and she got through it
with minimum problems
and a good deal of flair.

on her fourth day
just as they were about to have to redefine
their opinions of the opposite sex
she phoned in sick.

some of the controllers cheered
wasting no time at all
in getting out their old 'time of the month' jokes
laughing out loud about 'the painters being in'
as though this one day off
had confirmed their 'told-you-so' attitudes
about never being able to trust a woman
to do a man's job.

you could sense their relief,
they were not going to have to change
or redefine
anything
which after all
was just how they liked it.

hope

the new supervisor tells us that he wants us to fill in
internal 'big issue' forms
whenever we experience
or see things
that are going wrong
the new supervisor tells us that his door is always open
and will welcome any input we might have
on correcting the procedures
we currently have to follow
the new supervisor tells us
that he wants to foster a team
that has a no-blame culture
the new supervisor
is two months away
from becoming an old supervisor
but it will be a good two months
and you never know
some of us might decide
that the job isn't worth finding ways to kill ourselves
after all

Alex

after one too many bollockings
in front of the rest of the workforce,
after having his wages cut
for time off
even though he'd spent many hours after his shift before
helping out,
after being told he was on report
and had to ask a supervisor's permission
if it was okay for him to go and take a shit,
after being made to do three Saturday shifts a month
even though the rest of us
only had to do one every two,
after hearing that the new trainee controllers
were now being taken on
on the same pay he was getting
even though he had been there for over two years
and when he was told on a Friday
that he had to report to our new Waterloo office on Monday
even though he lived only half a mile
from our head office
he decided that he was being singled out
and took a spray can to all of the reps' and supervisors' cars
on the walk through the courtyard
outta there

we were once...

the 18-year-olds
come into the control room to learn the ropes
and sit next to the controller assigned to train them
doing everything that they tell them not to

the 18-year-olds come into the control room
and we tell them about this and about that
how they should never stamp their foot too hard
because the software will then crash
how they should be gentle with their keypad
because the hardware is as temperamental
as an old toaster
and how it is always better
to wait before you give out a job
because you never know what might be coming
around the corner

the 18-year-olds come into the control room
and no matter how much we tell 'em
they go around stomping their feet
and smashing at their keypads
allocating jobs to riders who shouldn't get them
as though it was the most important thing in their lives

and as we lean back in our controllers chairs laughing
we tell them that it is all okay
that we all understand
because all of us men
are 18-year-olds inside too
and for some unfathomable reason
will remain 18-year-olds
until the day we die

no enthusiasm

it was difficult for the trainee controllers
to stump up any enthusiasm
for a job that even if they made the grade
would yield a wage of only £400-per-week take home
with statutory sick pay
and two-weeks-a-year paid holiday thrown in
especially when they saw us veteran controllers
continuously getting our bonuses stopped by the supervisors
for running late on jobs
that needn't have run late
if only we had a hardware and software system
that could cope

it was difficult for the trainee controllers
to stump up any enthusiasm for the job
while the company made such a big thing
of taking on 65-grand-a-year sales reps
and in motivation meetings
had the front to say that it was 'them'
who they considered the future-blood
of the company

some of them didn't learn though

some of them actually put their name down on the dotted line
and committed to becoming a controller

lack of enthusiasm
was well known
as being the most valued commodity
if you wanted to be offered a long term controller's position
at Phoenix Express

the trainee controllers

in the prime of their lives
with faces that have never shaved
with minds that have never been unable to sleep
with hearts that have never skipped a beat
wearing £120 trainers
carrying glory in their bones
throwing around big ideas
about their undiscovered bands
about the paintings they are about to paint
and the poems they are about to write
walk around the control room
the first week of every new induction period
as though they can swallow fire

by the second week
there are fewer
wanting to do it their way
or
swallow fire

by the third week
there are normally only one or two left
and neither of them are interested in paintings or poems or
swallowing fire

only one every three-month cycle of our training programme
yields a trainee
who is willing or able
to stick it out

there is a lot to be said
for the morons who created Phoenix Express' training programme

any higher a success rate
and the future of art and revelation
might be placed in serious jeopardy

learning the ropes

having to work
on a radio where the volume can't be controlled
so the riders voices bang into your head
like ears rested against a big church bell for 10 hours
having to work
with software written in Mickey Mouse language
having to work
next to Hitler
or sat in a cavalcade
passing a grassy knoll
having to work
in constant chill
because the air conditioning thermometer has given up
and can't be switched off
until the engineer comes
which is like waiting
for love to come
having to work
next to men who hate your guts
having to work
next to men whose guts you hate
having to work
with hardware
that would have trouble
contributing to the launching of a motorised duck
gets to the new controllers

but they soon learn not to take it so seriously
they soon learn
that you being the only one that gives a damn
is recipe for madness

our Robbie

Robbie used to come in every day exactly one hour before
his shift started
and no matter what the weather
he'd always be dressed in jeans and a t-shirt
plonk his 24-stone frame
down into his controller's chair
and proceed to the read *the Guardian*
from back to front.
he had this ability
of being able to make everyone else within his vicinity
feel completely separate
from what was going on inside his head.
he used to have printed on his t-shirts
cartoon characters in various forms of distress
or stills from *The Rocky Horror Picture Show.*
when he was controlling
he kept it tight
and never took any risks
but whenever it got too busy for him
he used to spread himself out all over the place
and begin muttering to himself
before finally excusing himself
and going outside
to try and calm himself down.

the t-shirt that made us all finally realise it though
was the red one
with the picture of a broken-open skull
and all these marbles pouring out of it
with the words 'I'VE LOST MY MARBLES' printed underneath.

it was going to be a brave supervisor
who was going to have to tap Robbie on the shoulder
and tell him that he couldn't dance anymore
that was for sure.

states of sanity

my right-hand man
sat there next to me in his 24-stone-frame
flailing through his shifts
waving his scarred arms about and going outside
once every hour
just to calm himself down
continually trying to keep a lid on himself
because even he was unsure
what was in there.

from our once in a while whisky bouts
I knew that his mother and father
had been sectioned before he was 6
and that he'd been interfered with
coming through the many homes and foster parents
but the way he used to begin humming to himself
whenever it got busy
and the pressure got turned up
sitting there with his elbows on his knees
and his hands gripping his head
staring into the floor
before leaning back
into his controller's chair
and throwing up that favourite squeezy-ball of his
catching it smack in the middle of one of his big wrestler palms
so that it just disappeared
while over and over muttering to himself
that he was NOT going to end up like his ma and pa
NOT even if it killed him
made me not feel so paranoid
about the speed at which my life
seemed to be falling apart.

too hot to touch

the right-hand man
used to bring in a bag of Woolworth's Pic 'n' Mix
every day.

his favourites were the mini Black Jacks
but he also used to get through his fair share of
Drumstick lollies, Refreshers, Fruit Salads and
mini Toffee Crisp bars.
he used to roll up the used wrappers into little bullets
then elastic-band-them across the control room
trying to hit the backs of his fellow controllers heads
before convulsing into giggles
and revealing tons of black-stained teeth
every time he scored a hit.

no one used to complain about it though,
his 24-stone-frame and years spent in mental institutions
meant something to us.

so when the cleaner didn't turn up for a week
and the floor of the control room became literally covered
in bullet-shaped sweet wrappers
it was up to the supervisors
to have a word with our right-hand man
and tell him to use the various bins
dotted around the control room
that the rest of us had been ordered to use.

funny how a group of people
who pride themselves on administering authority and order
can think that it isn't actually so important
when confronted by a 24-stone 43-year-old
who eats Black Jacks and giggled like a demented kid
just because he was known to have served a 5-stretch
for the manslaughter of one of his foster dads
isn't it?

the lunatic

his having been released from a mental institution
fifteen-months before,
his relish in talking about
the way Hilda his pet python
squeezed the life out of the live rats he fed her before
'inching their deadness down her throat',
the way he continually sucked on Drumstick lollies
and pulverised his squeezy-ball
inside his big wrestler-palms
the whole day long,
the way he took down certain riders' addresses
who had called his abilities into question
by complaining directly to the supervisors
rather than first trying to sort it out with him,
the way he used to start pounding at his keypad
whenever it got busy
like he was trying to inflict serious pain on it
and the way he'd describe
while holding his hand up
with his thumb and first-finger less than a millimetre apart
how close he came last night
to actually killing himself
with his mad mad eyes boring into you
and all of his fat spilling out
made the rest of us controllers
think twice about refusing his invitation
to attend his six-month-old daughter's christening
at the Pig's Ear on Homerton High St
because we all knew
what rejection can mean
to a lunatic.

avoiding the big c

Lenny sat at his computer
telling anyone that would listen
about the times he'd spent in opium dens
in the hills around Chang Mai
half in and half out of consciousness
for 21-days solid.

Lenny never complained about the many times
his software crashed
or about the snail-speed of his interface card
which meant that every time he updated his screen
it would take at least 20 to 30 seconds
for it to re-boot
and reveal any new jobs
which caused him untold amounts of hassle
and often to miss crucial double-ups
which made everything run a bit later and later
and eventually
the supervisor to come out.

after he'd gotten his bollocking
he'd sarcastically offer the supervisor his chair
to see if he could do it any better
to which the supervisor would tell him to fuck-off
and to just get on with it.

none of the supervisors
ever took him up on his offer
because they knew
what Lenny already knew
which was that it could never be done
in the way it was supposed to be done
with what he had to work with.

Lenny new that there was nothing for it
than to get one of them new £500 interface cards
that could update a screen with its new jobs
faster than it took a lizard
to snap-shut its eye
and that that being out of the question
to never let yourself get drawn
into the realms of stress-related cancer.

corporate fashion victims

when we got the IBM account
the management set about developing the idea
that presentation was as important as service
if not more so

they sent many memos to the riders
asking them to clean up their act
and that they must wear the offered jackets
with the company logo
printed on its back

when it got back to them
that hardly any of the riders
were wearing the fuckers
they introduced a system
that stopped their £60 a week bonuses
whenever they were caught not wearing it

that the jackets weren't waterproof
let in the wind
and in bad weather
caused them to tremble
from the inside out
didn't seem to matter to them

only IBM did.

moody DR moody artist

once again Phil is burning threatening
to quit, move on, to someplace
where they'll recognise his quality and professionalism
and reward him thus.

he sits astride his XJ-900, helmet cocked on his head
staring into the ground between us
muttering.

I ask him how the new manager is doing for his band
but he is disinterested
mumbles something about supporting Supergrass
then continues with his threat to quit.

'any new songs?' I ask him.
'none lately,' he says.

then the controller calls him up on his radio.
he answers and gets a Bristol wait and return.
(about £140 for 5 hours work)

'what's that about quitting?' I ask.

he smiles at me
cracks his XJ-900 into gear
and roars off down the road.

he'll be alright for another week
and you never know
he might even get to write a few new songs.

it only mattered to Liam

Liam had a £750 Peugeot frame
that weighed in as much
as a dustbin-liner stuffed full of feathers

Liam had a pair of 80-pound-a-piece
Michelin tyres
and a Shimano break and gear set up
that was as close to the top end
as you could get

along with this
Liam wore a pair of Oakley tungsten's
and the loudest most noticeable
silks

he used to ride through the streets of Soho
feeling other
than all of the people moving around him

none of this, though
mattered to the cabbie
who whipped a well illegal uey
across Shaftesbury Avenue
laying his ton-plus cab
across the head-on-speed
of Liam's bike

and none of this mattered
to the surgeon
who apparently battled for 4 hours
trying to extract the pieces of metal
that had entered Liam's body
so that he could save his life

it only mattered
to Liam

keeping your sanity

the controllers listen intently to the couriers
in the pub across the road after a Friday shift
telling them that yet again their bonus has been stopped
for some reason or other
that had nothing to do with them
and that they're getting pissed off
with the shit that's being thrown at them
and the way they are being treated
every working day.

the couriers listen intently to the controllers
in the pub across the road after a Friday shift
telling them that yet again their bonus has been stopped
for some reason or other
that had nothing to do with them
and that they're getting pissed off
with the shit that's being thrown at them
and the way they are being treated
every working day.

no one with anything left in them
goes to the pub across the road
after a Friday shift

because they are too frightened that whatever's left
might be sucked clean away.

a bad bunch of spineless yellow men

if you didn't like the way things were going
or saw a problem potentially arising
you were encouraged by the supervisors
to fill out one of the internal complaint forms
which were kept in a red hardback folder
on a shelf above the desk
in the middle of the office

usually it was the supervisors
that made you not like how it was going
or it was your fellow controllers
who were the problems
potentially waiting to happen
which explained the quiet and piercing eyes
whenever somebody was seen
reaching up to the red hardback folder
that was kept on a shelf above the desk
in the middle of the office

in the three months since the process has been introduced
only 4 internal complaint forms
have been filed for further action
which just went to prove
that we have finally crossed over the line
and become
the spineless yellow bunch of men
we all thought we were

greased palm

Yankee Eight-Nine, a veteran courier of ours
is inside with the supervisor
wanting to know why his money has gone down since Christmas
by £130 a week.
the supervisor tells him that this is a fickle business
and while some weeks you can hit it off
there are others that leave you wondering
but that when you take the whole year into account
then he wasn't on such a bad screw
after all.
Yankee Eight-Nine is having none of it though
and tells the supervisor about Yankee Five-Eight
whose earnings apparently
have gone up by £100 per week
to which the supervisor says
that it is none of his business what other riders earn
but that he has made a mental note about it
and will talk to the controllers about his
situation
which he completely forgets about
the moment Yankee Eight-Nine
walks out of his office.

it was going to prove
the best use of two £50 notes
Yankee Five-Eight
had ever slipped into a Christmas card.

the definition of a circle

when Manni shot himself in the wrists
the rest of us were in bed
sleeping off drunks

when Peter
our old car controller
got caught interfering with his step-daughter
the rest of us were in bed
sleeping off drunks

when Tracy the telephonist
got beaten to a pulp by her boyfriend
the rest of us were in bed
sleeping off drunks

when our own women
cry out in the night
for lack of love lack of meaning
we are in our bed
sleeping off drunks

and people wonder why when we wake up
we can't wait to get drunk again

there there

at Manni's cremation
Phoenix Express didn't send a representative
but they did send a lovely wreath of yellow lilies
with a note attached.

'To Manni,
with our condolences,
from the management of Phoenix Express.'

the management at Phoenix Express
were notoriously known for talking to their employees
as though they didn't know or care
whether they were alive or dead.

when you step outside after your Friday shift

it is like the scent
of a fifteen-hundred-pound-a-night whore
it is like
dolphin's whooping and hollering in the bay
it is like stealing
a fat plumb
with time enough to squeeze it to bits in your hands
it is like when you were 7 again
striding along the canal
after an argument with your mum
totally convinced that you can deal with the dark
and are never going back again

when you step outside after your Friday shift
it is like the sound a bomb makes
just after it's been diffused
and the ticking has stopped
with 1 second left on the clock
it is like all the walls in all the world
suddenly falling down
and no one able to find any clothes
it is like too much goodness enough
to make a man seek ways
to kill himself
or the spell of a witch
finally kicking in
and the root-red stopper
torn from your heart
with all the wild blood
everywhere

terror street

why must we move mountains
just to hold down council flats
so that the roof
isn't ripped from us?
why must we be scared of the changing winds
stuff our mouths full of cotton-wool
just so they can't get in
and freeze our guts?
why must we go to bed fearing the day
only to mumble over and over ourselves to sleep
that we don't?
why must we sit in armchairs
sipping at dead wine in half-dead dark?
why must we walk through parks looking up at the sky
feeling nothing?
why must we pretend to believe
in the 50,000 times a day
rather than in the 50,000 times a day
that we don't?
why must we believe in protecting our jobs
when the sea
doesn't believe in anything?

where the greats have ended up

the majority of controllers
can't afford to be as weak as the machines
they have to rely on to keep their jobs.
if ever they develop a software problem
and have to phone in sick
a day's money is stopped them
and if ever they develop a hardware problem
the company will lay them off
the day before statutory sick-pay kicks in.

you have to be able to function under any circumstances
or at least be able to ride trophy hangovers
if you wanted to keep down a controlling job.

stories abound
about Super-Controllers,
men who once ruled the airwaves,
who once had families and flats,
cars and holiday homes,
but who have now lost their minds
and now sit dribbling in gutter-pubs
with 18-day beards
or on their own
in bedsits
with the phone unplugged
riddled with stress-related cancers
eating cold baked beans
and drinking cheap rose wine.

it is amazing how this company
is allowed to go on
making so much money
when its machinery and policies
of no sick pay and zero tolerance
has had and done away with
so many of the greats.

all of the drunken defeated men

all of the men in all of the alleyways
who once worked in control rooms or workshops
where they had to listen to 3-inch-high supervisors scream at them
until they had pumped themselves up so
they could feel as though they were
8-feet-tall
all of the men slumped in all of the shop doorways too drunk
to make it home who once tried to hold down a job
where they had to lump 45lb boxes of frozen lamb
into the backs of trucks for £8-per-hour before tax all of the men in
  all of the gutters
who had to juggle 6am drunks with clocking on at 9 for more years
than you would believe all of the men
at the bottom of their rivers who now have to wash cars or move
the contents of houses for men they consider
not to be men all of the men
who needed to kill themselves to free themselves of the pain of being
  men but couldn't
because they were all too men all of the men
angry and bitter that their principles and strength
were not enough to keep their women in love with them all of the men
who once batted their eyelids free of sleep and got up
feeling thirsty and invincible who now
find themselves walking around their bedsits at 4am
unable to sleep
trying to work out why
they feel like they are the only ones left

last rites

the look of laid-off 53-year-old men
unable to stop the tears
welling up inside their battered eyes the sight
of their broken bodies
walking out into the sun
for the last time the stink
of death as they start to split mocking us
still employed controllers that at least
they are now free again the pain
ripping them up the three kids and woman
they haven't told yet the nine years left
on their mortgage and endowment payments
the collection
handed over in a manila envelope and the hurt
and utter uselessness they try to block out
as they buy large tequilas for everyone
in the pub across the road waiting
for the last of the last bells to arrive
and everyone to walk away
from them this time
for good

3-parts water 8-parts paste

Horse was the unnamed leader of the Cunt Gang.
they had tons of open-cunt-shots
nail-gunned to their workshop walls.
Horse's office was covered from floor to ceiling
with phone-box flyers
interspersed with the occasional technicolor close up
ripped out of one of his many hard core magazines.
every now and then
one or some of the Cunt Gang
would infiltrate the thelephonists toilets
and nail-gun scores of open-cunt-shots
into the backs of the cubicle doors.
there would be a great furore
and the head supervisor would eventually call Horse up to his office
and tell him to get his troops
under control.

as the unnamed leader of the Cunt Gang
he escaped all definite blame
but nevertheless was thought responsible
for the 30-odd double-paged cunt-shots
found plastered the day after the meeting
over the windows of the supervisors' cars
in 3-parts water
and 8-parts paste.

time of the month

last Halloween
the mechanics raided the tampon bin in the telephonists toilets
and threaded each used one
through a piece of string
each divided by an apricot pumpkin-face
that they eventually wrapped around the hand rail
lining the steps connecting the workshop
to the operations floor.

from the light fitting
at the top of the staircase
they hung an 8lb pumpkin
with a carved out face
that had two blood-dark tampons shoved into its eyes
and a sanitary towel saturated with puss-yellow discharge
dangling out of its mouth.

they also had taken the trouble
to purchase a set of fairy lights
which they weaved
in and around
all of their art.

everyone condemned the act
as secretly
the bit that was born to be a mechanic in all of us
laughed its bloody head off.